W9-BMZ-793

EXPLORE THE UNITED STATES
ALABAMA

Sarah Tieck

Big Buddy Books

An Imprint of Abdo Publishing
abdobooks.com

Whiting Public Library
Whiting, Indiana

abdobooks.com

Published by Abdo Publishing, a division of ABDO, PO Box 398166, Minneapolis, Minnesota 55439. Copyright © 2020 by Abdo Consulting Group, Inc. International copyrights reserved in all countries. No part of this book may be reproduced in any form without written permission from the publisher. Big Buddy Books™ is a trademark and logo of Abdo Publishing.

Printed in the United States of America, North Mankato, Minnesota
102019
012020

THIS BOOK CONTAINS
RECYCLED MATERIALS

Design: Aruna Rangarajan, Mighty Media, Inc.
Production: Mighty Media, Inc.
Editor: Liz Salzmann

Cover Photograph: Shutterstock Images
Interior Photographs: AP Images, pp. 18, 19, 20, 28 (top); Butch Dill/AP Images, p. 14 (inset); chas53/ iStockphoto, p. 28 (bottom); GENE HERRICK/AP Images, p. 13; JOE HOLLOWAY JR./AP Images, p. 22; Library of Congress, p. 21; nickkurzenko/iStockphoto, p. 30 (middle); NYWTS/Wikimedia Commons, p. 27 (top left); Picasa/Wikimedia Commons, p. 23; Shutterstock Images, pp. 4, 5, 6, 7, 9 (all), 10, 11, 14, 16, 17, 18 (inset), 24, 25, 26 (top right), 27 (bottom), 28 (middle), 29 (all), 30 (top left, top right, bottom); Veni/iStockphoto, pp. 14, 15; Wikimedia Commons, pp. 26 (bottom left), 27 (top right)

Populations figures from census.gov

Library of Congress Control Number: 2019943184

Publisher's Cataloging-in-Publication Data
Names: Tieck, Sarah, author.
Title: Alabama / by Sarah Tieck
Description: Minneapolis, Minnesota : Abdo Publishing, 2020 | Series: Explore the United States | Includes online resources and index.
Identifiers: ISBN 9781532191046 (lib. bdg.) | ISBN 9781532177774 (ebook)
Subjects: LCSH: U.S. states--Juvenile literature. | Southeastern States--Juvenile literature. | Physical geography--United States--Juvenile literature. | Alabama--History--Juvenile literature.
Classification: DDC 976.1--dc23

CONTENTS

ONE NATION

The United States is a diverse country. It has farmland, cities, coasts, and mountains. Its people come from many different backgrounds. And, its history covers more than 200 years.

Today the country includes 50 states. Alabama is one of these states. Let's learn more about Alabama and its story!

DID YOU KNOW?

Alabama became a state on December 14, 1819. It was the twenty-second state to join the nation.

Alabama's natural areas include thick forests.

CHAPTER 2

ALABAMA UP CLOSE

The United States has four main regions. Alabama is in the South.

Alabama has four states on its borders. Tennessee is north. Georgia is east, and Mississippi is west. Florida and the Gulf of Mexico are south.

Alabama has a total area of 52,420 square miles (135,767 sq km). About 4.9 million people live there.

Puerto Rico became a US commonwealth in 1952.

DID YOU KNOW?

Washington, DC, is the US capital city. Puerto Rico is a US commonwealth. This means it is governed by its own people.

★ Regions of ★
the United States

West
Midwest
South
Northeast

CANADA

WASHINGTON
OREGON
MONTANA
NORTH DAKOTA
SOUTH DAKOTA
IDAHO
WYOMING
MINNESOTA
WISCONSIN
MICHIGAN
NEW HAMPSHIRE
VERMONT
MAINE
PENNSYLVANIA
MASSACHUSETTS
NEW YORK
RHODE ISLAND
CALIFORNIA
NEVADA
UTAH
COLORADO
NEBRASKA
IOWA
ILLINOIS
INDIANA
OHIO
CONNECTICUT
NEW JERSEY
DELAWARE
MARYLAND
WASHINGTON, DC
WEST VIRGINIA
VIRGINIA
SOUTH CAROLINA
ARIZONA
NEW MEXICO
KANSAS
MISSOURI
KENTUCKY
TENNESSEE
NORTH CAROLINA
OKLAHOMA
ARKANSAS
ALABAMA
GEORGIA
TEXAS
PACIFIC OCEAN
MEXICO
MISSISSIPPI
LOUISIANA
FLORIDA
ATLANTIC OCEAN
Gulf of Mexico
ALASKA
HAWAII
PUERTO RICO

N
W E
S

CHAPTER 3

IMPORTANT CITIES

Montgomery is Alabama's capital. It is also the state's second-largest city, with 198,218 people. It was an important place during the American Civil War. Later, many civil rights movement events happened there.

Birmingham is the largest city in Alabama. It is home to 209,880 people. This city is in a valley at the base of mountains. It grew as railroads were built.

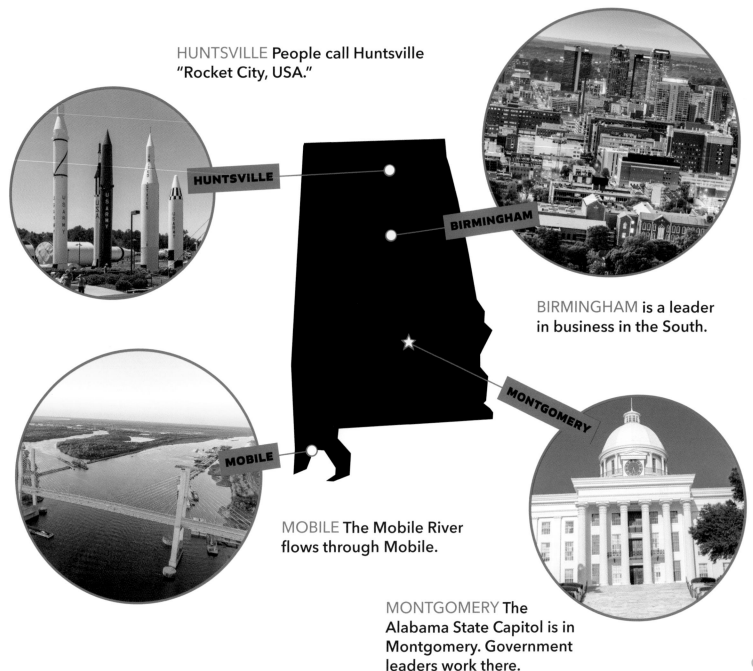

HUNTSVILLE People call Huntsville "Rocket City, USA."

HUNTSVILLE

BIRMINGHAM

BIRMINGHAM is a leader in business in the South.

MONTGOMERY

MOBILE

MOBILE The Mobile River flows through Mobile.

MONTGOMERY The Alabama State Capitol is in Montgomery. Government leaders work there.

9

The Mobile River empties into
Mobile Bay on the Gulf of Mexico.

Mobile is one of the oldest US cities. It was founded by the French in 1702. This city is on Mobile Bay. It is Alabama's only major city on a seaport. It is home to 189,572 people.

Huntsville is another important city in Alabama. It is known for space flight and missiles. Both the US Space and Rocket Center and NASA's George C. Marshall Space Flight Center are in Huntsville.

DID YOU KNOW?
Monte Sano Mountain is in Monte Sano State Park just outside Huntsville.

Monte Sano means "mountain of health" in Spanish.

CHAPTER 4

ALABAMA IN HISTORY

Alabama's history includes farming, war, and the civil rights movement. Native Americans lived on the land for thousands of years. European settlers started arriving in the 1700s. Many of them began farming cotton. By the 1830s, cotton had become an important crop.

Slaves worked the cotton fields for landowners. After the American Civil War, they were freed. But by the 1950s, African Americans were still treated unfairly. The civil rights movement helped change this. Martin Luther King Jr. was one of the movement's leaders.

King (*right*) was arrested while working for civil rights in Montgomery in 1956. He became known worldwide for his work as a civil rights leader.

CHAPTER 5

ACROSS THE LAND

Alabama has forests, mountains, swamps, and beaches. The Mobile River is in southern Alabama. At Mobile Bay, it empties into the Gulf of Mexico.

Many types of animals make their homes in Alabama. These include deer, owls, and hawks. Humpback whales are found off the coast in the Gulf of Mexico.

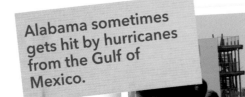

Alabama sometimes gets hit by hurricanes from the Gulf of Mexico.

DID YOU KNOW?

In July, the average high temperature in Alabama is 90°F (32°C). In January, it is 54°F (12°C).

Birds take flight from the Wheeler National Wildlife Refuge in Decatur, Alabama.

EARNING A LIVING

For many years, Alabama was a farming state. Cotton was the most important crop. People even called it "King Cotton."

Today, Alabama has farms that grow many crops. It is also a service and manufacturing state. It produces cars, paper, and foods. Many people also work in health care and retail jobs.

Chickens and other poultry have become important farm products in Alabama.

Farming cotton and other crops is still an important part of Alabama's economy.

CHAPTER 7
SPORTS PAGE

Hank Aaron is one of Alabama's sports stars. Aaron was born in Mobile in 1934. He played Major League Baseball from 1954 to 1976. Aaron is one of baseball's best hitters of all time.

When many people think of Alabama, they think of NASCAR. That's because the state is home to the Talladega Superspeedway. It is the longest NASCAR track!

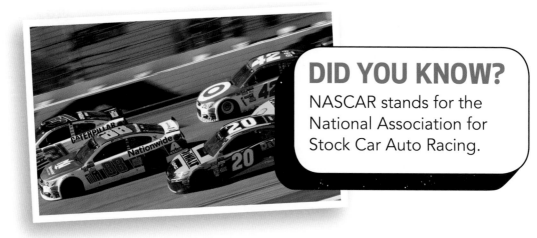

DID YOU KNOW?
NASCAR stands for the National Association for Stock Car Auto Racing.

Aaron hit 755 home runs
during his baseball career.

CHAPTER 8

HOMETOWN HEROES

Many famous people have lived in Alabama. Helen Keller was born in Tuscumbia in 1880. Around 1882, she became deaf and blind after a sickness.

In 1887, Keller started working with a teacher named Anne Sullivan. Sullivan taught her to read and write. This changed Keller's life. She grew up to be a speaker and author.

DID YOU KNOW?
Harper Lee is another famous author from Alabama. She wrote the book *To Kill a Mockingbird*.

Famous author Mark Twain called Sullivan (*right*) a "miracle-worker" for teaching Keller (*left*) to read and write.

Rosa Parks was born in Tuskegee in 1913. She became a civil rights movement leader. In 1955, Parks chose not to give up her bus seat to a white person. She was taken to jail for this. But, her choice helped change life for many Americans.

Paul William "Bear" Bryant was not born in Alabama. But, he coached the University of Alabama football team from 1958 to 1982. The team won six national titles under Bryant's leadership.

DID YOU KNOW?
Bryant was famous for wearing a checked fedora hat during Alabama games.

A Montgomery police officer takes Parks's fingerprints after her arrest in 1955.

CHAPTER 9

A GREAT STATE

The story of Alabama is important to the United States. The people and places that make up this state offer something special to the country. Together with all the states, Alabama helps make the United States great.

Gulf State Park is on the Gulf of Mexico.

Alabama's varied landscapes and culture make it a great US state!

TIMELINE

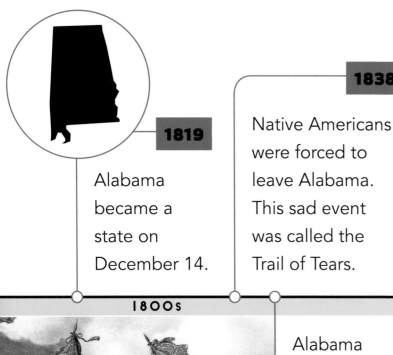

1819

Alabama became a state on December 14.

1838

Native Americans were forced to leave Alabama. This sad event was called the Trail of Tears.

1896

George Washington Carver was hired to run the agriculture department at a school in Tuskegee. His ideas about peanuts and sweet potatoes changed farming in the United States.

1800s

Alabama joined the Southern states to fight in the **American Civil War**.

1861

Montgomery's citywide electric trolley streetcars were the first in the United States.

1886

1955

Martin Luther King Jr. and others said they would not use buses in Montgomery. This helped start the **civil rights movement**.

2005

Hurricane Katrina harmed Alabama's coast.

2017

The University of Alabama football team won its seventeenth national title!

1900s

2000s

Insects called boll weevils destroyed Alabama's cotton crop. Many families struggled to earn money. This changed the state's economy.

The George C. Marshall Space Flight Center opened in Huntsville.

1960

A set of tornadoes hit Alabama and several nearby states. It was the largest set ever recorded. At least 230 people in Alabama died.

2011

1915

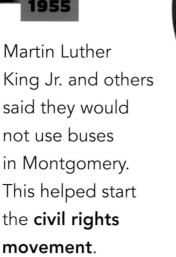

TOUR BOOK

Do you want to go to Alabama? If you visit the state, here are some places to go and things to do!

LISTEN

W.C. Handy was a famous blues musician from Alabama. In the 1900s, he became known as the Father of the Blues. Today, the W.C. Handy Music Festival is held every July in Florence, Alabama.

TASTE

Try some Southern food! Start the day with grits. Later, grab some fried chicken, sweet potatoes, and corn bread.

For dessert, pecan pie is an Alabama favorite.

CHEER
Catch a University of Alabama football game. The team's nickname is the "Crimson Tide."

The Alabama football team plays in Bryant-Denny Stadium in Tuscaloosa.

REMEMBER
Visit historic ships and airplanes at Battleship Memorial Park in Mobile.

DISCOVER
Learn about space travel at the US Space and Rocket Center in Huntsville. Some kids even attend space camp there!

Whiting Public Library
Whiting, Indiana

FAST FACTS

▶ STATE FLOWER
Common
Camellia

▶ STATE TREE
Longleaf Pine

▶ STATE BIRD
Yellowhammer

▶ STATE FLAG:

▶ NICKNAMES:
Cotton State, Yellowhammer State

▶ DATE OF STATEHOOD:
December 14, 1819

▶ POPULATION (RANK):
4,887,871
(24th most-populated state)

▶ TOTAL AREA (RANK):
52,420 square miles
(30th largest state)

▶ STATE CAPITAL:
Montgomery

▶ POSTAL ABBREVIATION:
AL

▶ MOTTO:
"We Dare Defend Our Rights"

GLOSSARY

American Civil War—the war between the Northern and Southern states from 1861 to 1865.

capital—a city where government leaders meet.

civil rights movement—the public fight for civil rights for all citizens. Civil rights include the right to vote and freedom of speech.

diverse—made up of things that are different from each other.

hurricane—a tropical storm that forms over seawater with strong winds, rain, thunder, and lightning.

region—a large part of a country that is different from other parts.

retail—the business of selling goods to people who will use them.

slave—a person who is bought and sold as property.

ONLINE RESOURCES

Booklinks
NONFICTION NETWORK
FREE! ONLINE NONFICTION RESOURCES

To learn more about Alabama, please visit **abdobooklinks.com** or scan this QR code. These links are routinely monitored and updated to provide the most current information available.

INDEX